Listening Out Loud

Listening Out Loud

The Leadership Paradox

Randall Huntsberry, Ph.D.

iUniversity Press

San Jose New York Lincoln Shanghai

Listening Out Loud
The Leadership Paradox

iUniversity Press
an imprint of iUniverse.com, Inc.

For information address:
iUniverse.com, Inc.
5220 S 16th, Ste. 200
Lincoln, NE 68512
www.iuniverse.com

Cover from original woodblock by Glenn Diddel

ISBN: 0-595-17045-5

Printed in the United States of America

In memory of my father,
M.D. Huntsberry
September 2, 1913–September 9, 1998

Prologue

One day, a young man set out to find a venerable sage who was reputed to live on a distant mountain. After searching for many days, the young man found the sage sitting in his hut whittling on a stick. The young man, being very impatient to learn the old man's secrets, quickly made his quest known. He said that he wanted to know how to become a great and powerful leader. The old man kept whittling as if he had heard nothing. The young man blurted out his question again, this time a little louder. Again, the old man did not reply. During the long afternoon, the young man repeated his question several times, but to no avail. Finally, the old man put away his knife and looked at the young man. "What is the sound of a great and powerful leader?" he asked. The young man was dumbfounded, and could think of nothing to say. The old man began polishing his stick with a soft clothe. Not wanting to appear as foolish as he felt, the young man remained silent. Time passed. Suddenly, the old man shouted, "That's it!" and walked out into the garden smiling to himself.

1

If you listen
in order to help others,
you have a problem.
If you can solve it,
you may be of some use.

2

Listen carefully to the one-legged man
scratching what isn't there.
Value what drives him crazy,
even if it is a *lost cause*.

3

Listen without attachment.
Otherwise, you will have already
stopped listening.

4

Listen here and now.
Where else
would you be?

5
A leader laughs
when she catches herself believing
she is really listening.

6
A leader *excommunicates* no one.
She embraces heretics and
communes with sinners.

7
Lacking nothing,
listen
with *nothing* in mind.

8
Listen
even if you already know
WHAT
you're going to hear.
An actor never offers
the same performance twice.

9
Listen impartially.
Everyone is family.

10
Listen to the words
people share in common.
The angle
will blow you away.

11
Listen to understand,
not control.
That's all you can do anyway.

12
Because a leader is always vulnerable,
magicians make a living
getting him to listen
to the wrong hand.
At such times he simply says,
what a show!

13
How can you hear
if your ears are stuffed
full of yourself?

14
Learn from the powerless,
how they listen to survive.

15
A leader listens
with his stinking nose
to everyone's garbage.

16
As long as you are simply listening,
you are neither
agreeing nor disagreeing.

17
The secret of leadership is creating
no followers.

18
Last Stands
can get you killed.

19
When few are listening,
listen louder!

20
Labels distort what's happening
like a three piece suit.
Boxes are for dead things.

21
With an ax to grind,
you will generate docile servants
or rebellious children.

22
Perch on your neighbor's thought
gently like a spring butterfly.

23
Be curious, not judgmental.
A cat has nine lives.

24
A leader is a *devil's advocate*.
He seduces Eve and disrupts Eden.
He is most human.

25
Many have titles,
but few are leaders.
Better to arrive unannounced.

26
Listen to the waves,
even if they are
a fuzzy bundle of particles.

27
Creativity springs from listening
as if for the first time
to what you've already heard
a thousand times before.

28
Listen to the way things are related
and all extraneous baggage
will fall away
as if by magic.

29
Because what is is,
there is no necessity of choosing
between contradictory solutions.
Listen until you have no choice.

30
A leader is not envious.
She fills her empty self
with others.

31
When people beg for
guarantees,
all you can do is listen,
forever.

32
Do not seek a specific result.
Simply listen
and you will achieve
what is necessary.

33
A leader stakes no flag on the moon.
He shares the universe.

34
By listening,
a leader encourages others
to get off the beaten path,
blaze their own trail.

35
Listen to the problem
wholeheartedly,
not to theories
about how to solve the problem.

36
Having no knowledge,
a leader listens
for what is known.

37
A leader doubts
that words tell the whole story.
Heisenberg made the same point *scientifically.*
Uncertainty *seems* certain.

38
Always camp
in your neighbor's field.

39
Children mature
when they are listened to,
which may explain why so many adults
seem like children.

40
Calculate what works
for all the players in the game,
and others besides.

41
Listening,
like the low bow or open handshake,
proves
you have no hidden agenda.

42
Like Chuang Tzu,
a leader doesn't know if she is
a leader dreaming she is a butterfly,
or a butterfly dreaming she is a leader.

43
By listening, a leader exposes
the hyperactive boredom of modern life.

44

As long as you don't name it,
you'll have to keep listening
to figure out
what's really going on.

45

Achieve your identity
not by what you do,
but by what you do not.

46

Chase *Truth*
like Gandhi chased the British,
with a little *t* and a grain of salt.

47

A leader is able to listen
to the degree she has no desire
for personal gain.

48
Listen first of all
to *what is*,
not what should or might be.

49
Listen to the endings
inherent in every beginning,
and even more
to the beginnings
inherent in every ending.

50
By listening,
you will stumble into something
you never dreamed of.

51
Ordinary people may speak
up to 180 words per minute,
but they can listen
up to 800 words per minute.
Much mischief lurks in this discrepancy!

52

People are always reinventing the wheel
but it never comes out quite the same.
A leader listens to the difference.

53

Listen for the sake of listening.
The meek shall inherit the earth,
but only
if it's the last thing on their mind.

54

Subtract the *I* from *I listen*
and you have *listen*
with no subject, no object, no filters—
just *listen.*

55

A leader is the quiet-point
around which everyone speaks.

56

A leader is never the same
two conversations in a row.

57
Listen with a resolute sense of ignorance.
Remember that you do not know
what the other knows in her heart,
what the words really mean.

58
Listen even to the murderer,
not because you condone murder,
but because he may be
a human being.

59
Listen most attentively
to the least among you. Otherwise,
great wisdom may be swallowed up
by your enthusiasm for numbers.

60
A leader has peripheral hearing
just like the Buddha's peripheral vision.
She listens to the chorus,
not just the soloists.

61
When a leader listens,
she surrenders her solitude.
Then, there is no hiding place,
anywhere.

62
A leader can live
with just about anything,
even a whiny dog.

63
By listening, a leader helps others
convince *him* of *their* truth.

64
A leader admits,
even when I'm listening,
my head is jabbering
like a tree full of monkeys.
It's a regular coffee klatch.
It's a wonder any voice
can get a word in edgewise.

65
A leader seldom stumbles
over what isn't there.

66
A leader is predictably *unpredictable*,
like a hand clap in a silent room.

67
Be supple.
Rigor mortis gets you nowhere.
Stop listening
and you're dead.

68
A *leader* listens.
A *manager* speaks.
Some say, managers are born
from a failure of nerve.

69
A leader knows the enemy and *they are us.*
She blames no one.
She points her finger at the moon
and touches her own heart.

70
A leader never finishes the *job.*
He comes up short
or long.
He operates outside the box.
He throws sand everywhere.

71
A leader does not shoulder our burdens.
He has a bad back.

72
A leader is a chameleon.
By listening,
she matches her surroundings.

73
Listen to where others are going.
Play catch up.

74
Listening precludes *either/or* thinking.
Go for *both/and* if you must.
Otherwise, opt for *neither/nor*
and surprise everyone.

75
A leader is no seer.
He holds gently to his guide's elbow
and listens
to her going's on.

76
Perfect obedience derives
from fearful listening.

77
Do not try to pin others down.
Keep a headlock
on the larger meaning, the real purpose
of what's happening.

78
A leader cries profusely
peeling the paradoxical onion.
Still, it's better than solving
the wrong puzzle.

79
Listening is a spectator sport.
Cheer from the stands during the game,
and hug everyone afterwards—
win, lose or draw.

80
Without laughter,
you will be unable to listen.
The words will scorch your ears.

81
You can never listen
to the *same* person twice.
So, why prejudge *who* may turn up
or what they will say?

82
A leader is a source of electricity,
not light.
Through her keen listening,
others enlighten themselves.

83
Listen appropriately.
You can't drive a nail
with a screwdriver.

84
A leader has no children.
He listens to everyone
as if they were his own.

85
Listening
speaks louder than words.

86
Listen as if your life depends on it.
Surely it does.

87
It is difficult to listen standing
over someone, or
on the other side of a brick wall.

88
Listen closely
to what insecurity breeds—
heroes and villains,
rescuers and scapegoats.

89
Some days you will hear *particles*,
other times *waves*.
It just depends.

90
A leader cocks her ear
at the edge of every crowd.

91
Encourage others to steal your ideas.
Then, listen carefully
to see if they escape.

92
Refuse either/or options.
Have your cake and eat it too.

93
Listen to what is going on
and then tell the stories you hear.
Without storytellers,
ships will collide in the dark.

94

Listen to the *unintended consequences*.
Remember 3M's failed ribbon material
that became the failed
plastic cup for brassieres
that became the standard U.S. worker
safety mask.

95

Listen to failures more than successes
because those who succeed
are apt to freeze the frame,
while those who have failed
are already heading somewhere else.

96

Listen to the ragtag remnant.
Noah kept two of everything
and saved the world.

97
A leader is not afraid
to get his feet muddy.
He is always wandering around
with his boots off
listening to his feet
squishing in the ooze.

98
Leadership is only temporary.
After three days,
fish and house guests stink.

99
Worry only about dying,
and this as little as possible.
Anything else is of little consequence
and only gets in the way of listening.

100
Do not build pyramids.
A mummy can't hear anything
all wrapped up
inside an abandoned tomb.

101
If you surround yourself
with people who tell the *truth*,
you'll have something worth listening to.
If you surround yourself
with liars and cheats,
the same applies.

102
Listen to *unlearn* as much as to learn.
What you already know
is your greatest impediment.

103
You are not restricted
by how far you can walk in a day.
Listen to one creature
and travel the earth.

104
By listening, you disrupt
the equilibrium of the universe.
Unheard, nothing changes.

105
Take what you hear
not as *The Truth*
but rather as a means
of *relating*.

106
Listen to the verbs,
the *doing* words,
rather than the nouns,
the frozen facts.

107
A leader listens to local issues
with a stranger's curiosity.

108
A leader leads the way
by bringing up the rear.
By coming in last,
nothing escapes her attention.

109
After clarifying where things *are*,
ask, *where are we going?*
Don't hang onto the past
unless you're heading backwards.

110
Laugh a lot.
Forty-seven percent of the companies listed
among the Fortune 500 in 1980
were not listed in 1990.

111
Listen standing on your head.
This will force you to *listen up*.
Be ridiculous.
Eat others alive.
They will enjoy your feast.

112
Listen to what people *say* is going on.
It is.

113
Hold onto the question
until someone throws up
an answer.

114
A leader listens to the distortions
residing in words
and calls us back to the thing itself.
A lemon is a lemon
only if you bite it.

115
Listen with an *empty mind.*
In this way you will create a space
in which the world can happen.

116
Listen without reacting—
a modern day *unmoved mover.*

117
One and one
are two plus *and*.
The *and* changes everything.

118
Listen to the *dead words*
and the life they sustain.

119
Like a dancer,
learn every technique,
then leap out on your own.

120
Like a bystander,
listen to both sides, but take neither,
not even your own.

121
Listen to what is there, but even more
to what isn't.

122
A leader is able to listen
because he is empty,
like the hole in the center of a wheel.

123
Listen until what won't work
dies of exhaustion.

124
By listening,
a leader rides the ego of others.
He enjoys the countryside immensely.

125
Don't fix on one word.
Step back, take it all in.

126
Listen to the silence
surrounding what is being said.
Words always appear out of *somewhere*.

127
A leader neither wins nor loses.
She simply listens
to the game on the radio.

128
When you listen to all sides,
people will not waste their time
trying to please you.

129
A leader is a tireless midwife.
Afterwards mothers say,
I did it myself.

130
Listen with your ear
to the ground. From there,
you won't threaten anyone.

131
Forget your own speech
and nothing will go unsaid.

132
Listening,
a leader does not worry
about what might be happening
but isn't.

133
A leader who does not listen
flutters in the barnyard
like a headless chicken.

134
Listen until the other is exhausted.
Then, offer refreshments.

135
A human being listens to the fear
under every bureaucratic rock.

136
Align yourself with the *enemy*
and avoid head-on collisions.

137
Always listening,
a leader seems hesitant.
Others strive all the harder
to make up his mind.

138
Speaking with a leader
is like yelling
into a deep canyon.

139
By sharing himself openly,
a leader inspires others to speak
so that he might listen.

140
Listen with authority,
but wield none.

141
Because a leader is not full of herself,
she listens well.

142
A leader avoids telling others
what he is dying to tell them.
He listens in order to transform himself.

143
Listen to the thing itself,
not what others say.

144
Having no hopes,
listen *as if there were no tomorrow.*

145
Opening himself up,
a leader lubricates the conversation.
He says, *tell me more about you.*

146
Listen acutely to the assumptions
embedded in common sense.
Things seldom *go without saying*
or *stand to reason.*

147
Listen to the words
of a *rational* argument
even as you feel
the pulse of the speaker quicken.

148
Listen standing on one foot.
Maintain your balance
until you hear
the other shoe drop.

149
When you listen
without expectations,
you cannot fail.

150
Listen to the prejudices of others.
They may be your own.

151
In the stillness of your own silence—
the other's very breathing.

152
By listening,
a leader appears to be following,
which in fact he is.

153
Listen with *dead calm*.
In this way, you will never get lost
in the flurry.

154
Advance by withdrawing.
Surround the *enemy*
with your ears.

155
By listening, you learn
the *language* of others.

156
Couch your response.
Do not whistle into a strong wind.

157
Listen, because you know
when a person speaks,
he wants to be heard.

158
Because a leader does not struggle
to know anything,
she is able to hear
the forest in the trees.

159
Listen to what is intended.
Avoid the wrong fight.

160
Listen
by quieting
your own voices.

161
By listening, use others
as a means
to *their own* ends.

162
A leader is able to listen
because she does not aim
for yesterday's success.

163
Do not listen out of desire to foster
your own personal interests.
If it comes to this,
throw yourself overboard.

164
What makes a leader different
is that when he is listening,
he is *really* listening.
Simple as this is, it is more difficult
than ruling the world.

165
Listen because there is never
only one way
to do anything.

166
A leader always listens
from his neighbor's front porch.

167
Someone asks,
*what is the most important thing
to teach our children?*
A leader knows, a child is never not learning.
Get out of their way.

168
By listening,
you will remain yoked with your partners.
Pushing ahead or falling behind
will upset the wagon.

169
Listen to people, not problems.
In this way, you will discover
their solutions.

170
A leader does not expect
fish to fly,
but she also knows
she could be mistaken.

171
Listen most intently
to what others take for granted.
*Always count their chickens
before you hatch.*

172
By listening,
you will transcend the distinctions—
this or that,
you or me.

173
Listening to the vision of others
is a leader's vision,
but she need not mention it.

174
Listening is finally difficult
to the degree
you have a stake
in the practice of listening itself.

175
Emerson says,
it is a luxury to be understood.
So listen
and make everyone rich.

176
Listen to what others
own up to.
Possession is nine-tenths of the law.

177
Ask for help,
then listen.
The more dependent you are,
the more dependable others become.

178
Listen to understand,
not to prepare a stronger defense.
After all, what if the other guy is *right*?

179
Listen closely
with your bare hands.

180
Listen to the *multiple personalities.*
Do not expect consistency,
only surprises.
Predictability is a hopeless addiction.

181
Though you listen over
and over again,
do not expect to hear
the postman ring *twice.*

182
By listening to just one other person,
you hear the whole world.
Everyone
is heavily populated.

183
By listening, you discover
what counts
as *rational* to others,
and how varied
this universal has become.

184
By listening steadfastly to your opponent
you will discover
your own shadow.

185
A leader is a trickster.
She listens seriously
to laughter
and laughs when things are most serious.
She looks forward
to singing and dancing
at her own funeral.

186
Listen patiently for a revelation,
a *religious* experience.

187
To hear the unknown,
we must die to the known.
Because we are afraid to die,
we do not listen.

188
Listen with a sense of irony,
that even your own doubts
are doubtful.

189
A leader does not have to pretend
to be anything.
She *is*
simply listening.

190
Listen quietly
to the noisy world.

191
Listening, a leader does not favor
his own position.
He would rather limp.

192
Listen with missionary zeal,
but offer no salvation.

193
Be very careful
about the questions you ask.
A wrong question can only generate
a wrong answer.

194
Make the familiar strange,
like a fish listening
to the sound of the sea.

195
Listen without defensiveness.
Besides, what have you got to lose?

196
By listening, a leader assumes
the humble position.
Don't confuse this
with weakness or defeat.

197
Listen to the mind *and* the body,
especially poor Descartes'.

198
By listening, a leader signals
that he is not an enemy
lurking in the shadows.

199
Listen especially
to whatever gets in the way of your listening.
Even then, do not fight it.
Simply listen to yourself
not listening.

200
Because no one is capable
of pronouncing the last word on anything,
listen to everyone
no matter
their accent.

201
A leader learns how to listen
by being listened to
probably as a child.
Is this why we have so few leaders?

202
Listening is not a zero-sum project.
Nobody loses anything.

203
Listen to the *thing-in-its-context*,
not to the *thing-in-itself.*
Things are not nearly so distinct
as people once thought.

204
Listen to others reverently,
as if they were descended from gods.
Who knows?

205
A leader listens like an open book.
Nothing is *classified*.

206
By listening, you unleash
the full energy of others.
What a frenzy!

207
By listening, you *e-ducate* others,
which means you *lead* them *out*.
You most certainly do not
fill them up with yourself.

208
Listen playfully.
Afterwards, there will be no residue.

209
A leader listens moment by moment
without any ideology
to make him feel secure.

210
Listen quietly.
De-wheel the band wagon.

211
Listen to the eye of the hurricane
and you will not be blown away.

212
Avoid
the straight line of violence.
By listening,
encircle even the enemy.

213
Listening throws a bucket
of cold water on any fire.

214
Do not try to slay
the dragons of conflict.
Listen through the night
while they fall asleep
one by one.

215
Listen with a sense of futility,
as best you can.

216
By listening, *un-think* the thinkable.

217
Listen hopefully,
not that things will necessarily turn out well,
but that whatever happens
will somehow make sense,
even in its absurdity.

218
Listening intently
creates solidarity with others.
What you hear
is gravy.

219
A failed leader is one
nobody has talked to
lately.

220
A leader listens to people
make exaggerated claims,
then exaggerates
the exaggeration.

221
Listen to what is *left unsaid*,
the overtones
the undertones
the reverberations in the hills.

222
Listen today,
and then again tomorrow.
Sometimes, a clean shirt helps.

223
Be prepared for the possibility
that what others say
will make absolutely
no sense.
In such cases, ask to hear it again.

224
Listen, but cast no blame.
Scapegoats usually bear fleas
from the blamer's own dog.

225
Listen in *slow motion,*
faster than others can speak.

226
Because a human being is listening,
she is not a *listener*
or anything else.

227
Listen compassionately
to another's suffering
without making it or not making it
your own.

228
The last thing a leader wants to do
is listen.
He is human and would rather
have his own way.
But, as he listens, he forgets himself
and things fall into place.

229
If you should not
walk *blindly,*
you should not listen *deafly.*

230
Listen to the way things are,
not the way
you want them to be.

231
When a leader listens,
that's all she does.
She does not *walk and chew gum.*

232
Listen first to the concepts and labels,
then to the feelings
that drive them.

233
To be able to listen,
you must *see* yourself
listening.

234
Listen with the ears
of *Every*-Man-Woman-and-Child.
Do not be victimized
by your own breathing.

235
You cannot listen
fixated
on your own navel.

236
Listen as seriously
as you would play at any game.

237
Always listen to the dancer's eyes
as well as her feet.

238
A leader is consumed
with curiosity about the unknown.
Tell me more, he says, *even if it hurts*.

239
When you really listen,
speaker and *listener* disappear.

240
Listening, a leader is content
however things turn out.

241
By listening
to billions of twitching particles,
you participate
in the revision of *Eternal Truth*.

242
Always give to others
by *stealing*
what they have to say.

243
If you listen
without defensiveness,
no one can pull your trigger.

244
Listen carefully
to the paradoxes of life.
Find a way
to embrace
both horns of the dilemma.

245
By listening,
impersonate everyone.

246
Listen without attachment
to your own ruminations.
A leader has only one obsession,
which she can't remember.

247
A leader is an amateur, not an expert.
He owns, like Socrates,
his own great ignorance.

248
Drag your feet
when you notice in others
a loss of nerve.

249
Listen without additions or subtractions.
Be *simple-minded*—
a zero!

250
A leader listens with equanimity
to the good and the bad,
because such a difference
never *enters her mind.*

251
By listening to people just as they are,
a leader encourages everyone
to become what they are not.

252
A leader listens until *he* gets it straight.
Then, no one is confused.

253
Not listening makes a leader
uncomfortable,
like feeling a mote in his own eye.

254
Listen to what others forget to say,
what they take for granted
in all the hullabaloo.

255
With your eyes wide open,
listen to the bitter end.
*You don't know
what you don't know.*

256
It is easy to listen
on a quiet back road.
The real test is down on Main Street.

257
A leader is able to listen
because she is *possessed*
neither by fear nor desire.

258
If it takes *a whole village to educate a child*,
it takes a leader to listen to a whole village.

259
Be sensitive to your own *deaf spots*.
Ask for someone
to turn up the volume.

260
A leader listens spontaneously
because he has forgotten
how to listen.

261
Listening *single*-mindedly,
a leader generates *one*-ness
between factions.

262
A leader is a person
who really listens
to *herself.*

263
Because *a little knowledge
is a dangerous thing,*
listen on tiptoes
down to the last word.

264
By listening,
you will never defeat anyone.
But, you will never be defeated either.

265
Find out who someone is
by listening
to the uncertainty they bear.

266
A leader is like a gentle spring rain.
When he listens, others flower.

267
Listen with the eternal curiosity of a child,
not the *expert answers* of a parent.
Indeed, a leader is an *expert*
at not being a parent.

268
A leader listens to enlarge
his own understanding.
He is not teaching,
but being taught.

269
Listen in joyous anticipation
of hearing something new,
or something old.

270
Do not listen to parties or alliances,
but to the specifics of *what is*.
A leader takes sides
only with the thing itself.

271
A leader shatters
any image of herself listening.
She says, *I'm not made of dead stone.*

272
Because a leader is not anxious
about herself,
she is free to listen
to the anxieties of others.

273
Listen with marvelous awe
as if you were an astronaut
observing this lovely sphere
from outer space.

274
When you are listening,
others cannot refute
what you aren't saying.

275
By listening repeatedly,
a leader avoids
repeating himself.

276
As a man of leisure,
a leader has nothing better to do
than listen.

277
A leader would rather listen
than tell people what to do.

278
Because a leader is homeless
she listens to everyone on their own turf.

279
Listen until everyone hears
what they are saying
to themselves.

280
Listen in order to understand
what matters most to others,
not to persuade them *to do it your way.*
At worst, help others mobilize in the face
of *their* necessity.

281
Listen patiently to all complaints
and ask for detailed evidence
concerning every scapegoat.

282
Provide the field
so that others may plant.
Then wait patiently for spring.

283
In times of crisis,
be very careful about listening.
Tyrants emerge
when people are most afraid.

284
When a leader listens to others,
she lingers
on what's between them,
the space
where the gods are dancing.

285
Do not hesitate to listen.
Someone has to stop the ball rolling.

286
By listening, a leader generates trust.
Then, people tell her
what's really going on.

287
Listen with soft eyes
and your horse will vault
over the skies.

288
If you listen carefully
everything will change,
even your desire for certainty.

289
A leader *stirs the pot*
by mirroring the contradictions he hears
between words and actions.

290
A leader listens without measure.
She does not own a watch, scale or rule.
She asks those she meets,
how do YOU measure things?

291
Sometimes, a leader will hear
frustration and anger
at her refusal to provide *the* answer.
At such times, she listens steadfastly
until people are convinced
that she really has no answer.
Only then can she help look for one.

292
Listen without clever tricks.
Never *use*
direct eye contact.

293
A leader who truly listens
will start a revolution.

294
While he is listening,
a leader accepts the possibility
that he will appear
indecisive, lazy or cowardly.
At such times, he announces,
nap time.

295
By listening intently,
a leader draws everyone together
like scattered filings to a magnet.

296
Accept with courage
the danger inherent in listening—
that you might *get talked into something.*

297
A leader listens precisely
to the disruptive noises
others would tune out.

298
By listening, a leader *forces* others
to speak.

299
Listen to others as if they were
speaking in tongues.
Each person possesses a choir full of voices.

300
Because self-deception is his nemesis,
a leader listens especially to those
he would most like to silence.

301
By listening, a leader does not ask
for more than people can give.
Even the Israelites
needed forty years in the wilderness
before they could think like a free people.

302
After she asks a question,
a leader surprises everyone.
She actually listens to the answer.

303
Listen
because most people are afraid
that what they have to say
doesn't matter to anyone.

304
Listen to the accent,
not only the words.

305
A leader listens patiently
so that he doesn't get there
ahead of everyone else. Otherwise,
like Socrates, he might earn a stiff drink.

306
Listen to the other's story
without telling him
how it should end or what he should do.
Do not *create him in your own image*.
Only God does that.

307
If by listening
you could understand
one person completely,
you would lack nothing.

308
Listen like a sinner
for redemption,
not like a priest
for sin.

309
A leader is uncivlized.
She asks why
the emperor
is riding a naked horse.

310
By listening,
a leader conquers himself,
not others.

311
A leader celebrates
the infinite possibilities
inherent in his fundamental
ignorance.

312
Like the Japanese cook,
a leader blends the six tastes—
bitter, sour, sweet, hot, salty, plain—
into one harmonious meal.

313
Idolize no one,
especially yourself.

314
Draw your opponent
into the noonday sun
and his shadow will disappear.

315
There are no ear-lids—
except in your mind's eye.

316
A leader rides her horse
with soft eyes and heavy ears.

317
When someone tells you
that you are dead wrong,
take a deep breath
and put your stethoscope
to his heart.

318
Listen
all the more intently
to each *dumb* idea.

319
Like Heraclitus, a leader assumes
the way up and the way down
are one and the same.

320
Listen mostly
to what isn't being said.

321
Because we are what we practice,
by listening
you become *listening*.

322
No matter how much
a leader thinks she knows,
she always listens
with renewed amazement.

323
In a world
of uncertainty and doubt,
a leader does a whole world
of listening.

324
Listen to others
like an excellent horseman—
above the saddle,
no rider;
below the saddle,
no horse.

325
A leader's greatest challenge
is to stay
out of the way.

326
Because a leader listens so intensely,
people accuse her of staring.

327
It takes courage
for a leader to really listen
when he knows
it will blow his mind.

328
A closed mouth
really says something.

329
By listening intently,
a leader achieves things
even he never imagined.

330
When time is running out,
listen very slowly.

331
Put away
what is in your head
and listen
to what is actually happening.

332
When you really listen,
you leave no trace.

333
Never do unto others
what you wouldn't do
to your boss.

334
Walk when you walk,
sit when you sit,
wobble when you wobble.

335
To be able to listen,
you must be empty-headed.

336
Do not worry
about the contempt
familiarity breeds,
only the blindness.

337
A leader does not strike
a blind man
for knocking him down
or a deaf man
for not listening.

338
What you do not notice
becomes your life.

339
A leader listens in order to comprehend
the world as it is,
especially when she doesn't like
what she sees.

340
Iconoclasm is a desperate attempt
to deny the fact
that we have created our gods
in the first place.

341
A leader knows
there are at least ten rules
he should follow
to be most effective.
Fortunately,
he can't remember
a single one.

342
A human being is not a white male,
or anything else.

343
You will never learn to sing and dance
if you come from a land
where no one cries at funerals.

344
A leader stops listening
when he comes to believe
that his job is all important.

345
A smart captain does not
attempt to control the wind,
only the sails.

346
Choose freely,
then listen graciously
to the inevitable consequences.

347
A great leader's contribution—
a pair of fresh ears.

348
A leader succeeds
when he is not taken in
by himself.

349
By listening, a leader becomes clairvoyant.
She can predict the future
because she has heard all the voices.

350
Discover
what people really want to do,
then tell them,
Go do it!

351
A great leader
carries a big broom.

352
By listening first,
a leader does not abuse his power.

353
A leader listens
to what she hears,
then acts.

354
A leader succeeds
because he needs
so much help.

355
A leader listens
to the other side
of the moon

356
By listening,
a leader learns
from other's mistakes.

357
A leader listens to the bald man
with a fine-toothed comb.

358
Leadership is the superior power
of listening.

359
By listening,
a leader protects others
from his own ignorance.

360
Listen to everyone
as if they were an honored guest.

361
By listening,
the muddy water
settles by itself.

362
A leader listens
when she doesn't know,
and when she does.

363
Singing the blues,
a leader can listen
to just about anything.

364
By listening,
a leader allows others
to think.

365
A leader succeeds
by hearing the inaudible.

366
By listening,
a leader leads others
back to themselves.

367
A leader listens gently
because she knows
what she hates in others
may be herself.

368
Ponder life,
not as a problem to solve,
but as a mystery to live.

Epilogue

Many pupils were studying meditation under the Zen master Sengai. One of them used to arise at night, climb over the temple wall, and go to town on a pleasure jaunt.

Sengai, inspecting the dormitory quarters found this pupil missing one night and also discovered the high stool he had used to scale the wall. Sengai removed the stool and knelt in its place.

When the wanderer returned, not knowing that Sengai was the stool, he put his feet on the master's head and jumped down into the grounds. Discovering what he had done, he was aghast.

Sengai said: "It is very chilly in the early morning. Do be careful not to catch cold."

The pupil never went out at night again.

(Adapted from Zen Flesh, Zen Bones compiled by Paul Reps)

About the Author

Randall Huntsberry, Ph.D. is a corporate consultant, marriage and family counselor, and poet. Formerly, he was a college professor, modern dance improvisationist and oil field roustabout. He has his B.A. and Ph.D. from Harvard University.

www.ingramcontent.com/pod-product-compliance
Lightning Source LLC
Chambersburg PA
CBHW031240280526
45784CB00004B/1647